Toucan

KIDS EXPLORE!

Toucan

There are 40 different species of the Toucan. This bird has been used by many advertisers - probably because it is cute and a little weird looking. Even though you may not have guessed it, the toucan is closely related to the woodpecker. Why? It has to do with its tongue and toes, which we will learn more about later. In fact, we are going to explore many cool things about this creature. Like where it lives, its babies, its extraordinary abilities and so much more. Read on to be totally amazed with the toucan.

Where in the World?

Did you know this bird likes to live in the jungle? The toucan can be found in the rainforests of central and South America. It can be found in places in the Caribbean. This colorful bird can also been seen in many zoos around the world. It is a playful and fun character to watch.

The Body of a Toucan

Did you know this bird has shiny black feathers? It can also be decorated with bright whites, yellows, oranges, reds, and greens, depending on the species. This bird can grow from 11.5 inches long (29 centimeters) to 29 inches long (63 centimeters). It has a short compact body- a lot like a crow. Its neck is also short and thick and it has a rounded tail.

The Beak of the Toucan

Did you know the toucan is best known for its large colourful bill? Even though its bill is very large, it is also very lightweight. It is made up of a substance called, keratin (like our fingernails). The bill measures around half the toucan's body length. It is used more for eating, rather than fighting.

The Tongue of a Toucan

Did you know both toucans and woodpeckers have long tongues? The tongue of the toucan is very narrow and has bristles along the sides of it. This helps it to catch and to taste its food before swallowing it. Its close relative, the woodpecker, does the same thing.

The Toes of the Toucan

Did you know this bird is, zygodactylous? This means it has 2 toes pointing forward and 2 toes pointing backward. This provides the toucan with strength and stability when moving through dense branches. It can also move with ease up and down tree trunks, or in and out of tree cavities.

Toucan Locomotion

Did you know this bird does not need to travel long distances? Because all of its food and needs are right in the jungle, the toucan does need to move around a lot. In fact, the toucan's wings are actually quite small. This makes it not a great flyer and it can only fly in the air for short distances. This is where its cool feet come into play. The toucan just hops from branch-to-branch.

What a Toucan Eats

Did you know toucans are omnivorous? This means they will dine on both plants and meat. Toucans eat fruits, berries, nuts and seeds along with eggs, insects and small mammals. However, they eat mostly fruit that they can find in their area. They will start to eat fruit in the morning hours and even make long journeys to find fresh fruit.

The Toucan's Special Ability

Did you know the word "toucan" comes from the sound this bird makes? Their songs often resemble croaking frogs. They can also make barking, croaking and growling sounds. They can even bray like a donkey. And just like humans, female toucans usually have a higher voice than the males.

The Toucan's Nest

Did you know the Toucan builds its nest in trees? This bird calls a hollowed-out tree cavity home. It builds its nest here to keep it safe from predators. In fact, the toucan even has a hard time getting into its nesting-hollow. It has to turn its head backwards and tuck its bill under a wing.

Toucan Mom and Dad

Did you know the mom toucan usually lays around 3 eggs? Both male and female toucans make good parents. After the chicks hatch the dad toucan helps the mom feed the babies. He will also help defend the nest against predators.

Baby Toucans

Did you know toucan chicks are born with small bills? Their bills will not fully grow in for a few months. Newborn toucans are born blind and featherless. By 3 weeks-old their eyes will open and they will sprout little feathers. They stay in the nest for 6 to 8 weeks.

Predators of the Toucan

Did you know this bird has many natural predators? Toucan eggs are hunted by weasels, snakes, cats and rats. The adult toucan can be taken by forest eagles, hawks, owls, boas, jaguars and margays. Humans have also hunted the toucan for the pet trade.

Life of a Toucan

Did you know the toucan can live up to 12 years in the wild? Once baby toucans are fully grown they have a better chance at living a long time. Captive toucans in zoos can live to be 20 years-old. In the wild, toucans are noisy and social birds. They will travel in small flocks of around 22 individual birds.

Toco Toucan

Did you know this toucan has thin blue skin around its eyes? This blue skin is surrounded by another ring of bare, orange skin. The body of this beauty is mainly black. It has a white throat and chest. It can measure from 22 to 26 inches (55 to 65 centimeters) and it weighs about 1.93 pounds (876 grams).

Keel-billed Toucan

Did you know this toucan has a colorful bill? The Keel-billed Toucan ranges in length from around 17 to 22 inches (42 to 55 centimeters). Its large bill alone measures around 6 inches in length (15 centimeters). It has beautifully colored feathers, as well.

Quiz

Question 1: What other bird is the Toucan like?

Answer 1: The Woodpecker

Question 2: The toucan has a short compact body. What other bird is that like?

Answer 2: The crow

Question 3: The toucan is *zygodactylous*. What does that mean?

Answer 3: It has 2 toes facing frontward and 2 toes facing backward.

Question 4: Which parents help raise the chicks?

Answer 4: Both mom and dad toucan rear the young

Question 5: Why do humans hunt the toucan?

Answer 5: For the pet trade

Thank you for checking out another title from Kids Explore! Make sure to check out Amazon.com for many other great books.

Made in the USA
Monee, IL
26 February 2020